GrowForth Kids Co.

LET'S START A BUSINESS!

Your First Steps into Entrepreneurship

I0560791

Matthew MacMillan
and Scott MacMillan

GROW FORTH
PRESS
—BY GRAMMAR FACTORY—

Grow Forth Kids
MacMillan Company Limited
25 Telegram Mews, 39th Floor, Suite 3906
Toronto, Ontario, Canada
M5V 3Z1

www.growforthpress.com

MacMillan, Matthew and Scott MacMillan
GrowForth Kids Co: Let's Start a Business! Your First Steps into Entrepreneurship / Matthew MacMillan and Scott MacMillan.

Paperback ISBN 978-1-998528-58-5
Hardcover ISBN 978-1-998528-60-8
eBook ISBN 978-1-998528-59-2

1. JNF013050 JUVENILE NONFICTION / Business & Economics / General.
2. JNF013030 JUVENILE NONFICTION / Business & Economics / Personal Finance.
3. JNF000000 JUVENILE NONFICTION / General.

Production Credits
Book production and editorial services by Grammar Factory (www.grammarfactory.com)

Contents

Introduction: Welcome to GrowForth Kids Co.   1

PART 1: GETTING STARTED
Turn your big idea into a real business you can launch

1. **Ideation:** Coming up with smart business ideas from what you enjoy   4
2. **Validation:** Finding out if people want what you're offering   6
3. **Selection:** Picking the best idea to turn into a business   8
4. **Ideal Customer Profile (ICP):** Who your business is for – and why   10
5. **Startup Capital:** How much money you need – and how to get it   12

PART 2: SHAPING YOUR OFFER
Design what you're going to sell – and get ready to test it

6. **Offers:** What you'll sell and how it's put together   16
7. **Unique Selling Proposition (USP):** What makes your business stand out   18
8. **Pricing:** How much to charge – not too high, not too low   20
9. **Minimum Viable Product (MVP):** Start small and test your idea early   22
10. **Break-Even Point:** When you've made enough to cover your costs   24

PART 3: LAUNCHING AND RUNNING YOUR BUSINESS
Show your business to the world – and start helping your customers

11. **Branding:** Pick a name, look, and style people remember   28
12. **Marketing:** Help people find your business and get curious   30
13. **Sales:** Turning "Maybe" into "Yes!" the friendly way   32
14. **Customer Satisfaction:** Keep your customers happy and coming back   34
15. **Procurement:** Get what you need to make or do what you sell   36

PART 4: IMPROVING AND GROWING
Make your business better, stronger, and ready to grow

16. **Operations:** Keep things running smoothly behind the scenes   **40**

17. **Goals:** Set smart goals and track your progress   **42**

18. **Innovation:** Add new ideas or offers to grow   **44**

19. **Scaling:** Reach more people with what you've built   **46**

20. **Word of Mouth (Referrals):** Let happy customers spread the word   **48**

Business Brain Challenge
Can You Launch a REAL Business?   51

BACK POCKET BONUSES

"What I Tried" Log   **56**

Certificate of Completion   **67**

Glossary: Big Words Made Simple   **69**

A Thank-You from GrowForth Kids   **71**

Behind the Book: Meet the Authors   **73**

Introduction

Welcome to GrowForth Kids Co.

Hi there, Business Brain! 👋 We're so glad you're here.

At GrowForth Kids Co., we believe that big ideas can start small – and that kids like you have everything it takes to build something amazing.

You might be wondering: **"Can I really start a business?"**

The answer is YES. Not someday. Not when you're older. Right now.

You don't need a fancy office, a big loan, or a team of grown-ups. All you need is a spark – an idea you care about, a plan to make it happen, and the courage to give it a try.

That's what this book is all about.

We'll walk you through everything you need to know to start a real business – whether you're selling lemonade, pet-sitting for neighbors, designing stickers, or inventing something brand-new.

Inside, you'll learn:

- How to come up with and choose a great business idea
- How to design what you're selling (and who it's for)
- How to find customers and make your first sales
- How to keep your business running – and even grow it over time

Each chapter explains one important idea, with real examples and simple language. And just like in the other GrowForth Kids Co. books, you'll find a Try This! section at the end of every chapter to help you take action right away.

By the end of the book, you'll be ready for your biggest challenge yet: Launching a REAL business. It can be something small. Something creative. Something helpful. Whatever you choose, it'll be yours. And that's where the magic begins!

Ready to start? Let's grow forth.

Part 1

Getting Started

Turn your big idea into a real business you can launch

"You don't have to be great to start, but you have to start to be great."

— Zig Ziglar, speaker and sales expert

Every great business starts the same way: With an idea.

It could be something fun. Something helpful. Something that solves a problem or makes someone's day a little better.

In this part of the book, you'll learn how to spot those ideas, test them out, and turn your favorite one into a real plan.

You'll figure out how to:

- Come up with business ideas from things you already enjoy *(Ideation)*
- Find out if people actually want what you're offering *(Validation)*
- Choose the best idea to turn into your first real business *(Selection)*
- Figure out who your business is really for – and what they care about *(Ideal Customer Profile)*
- Know how much money you need to get going – and where you might find it *(Startup Capital)*

This is the "thinking and planning" stage – and it's one of the most exciting parts of being an entrepreneur. Why? Because it's where anything is possible.

You don't have to get everything perfect. You just have to start.

So grab a notebook, a pencil, and your Business Brain.

Let's get your idea off the ground.

1

Ideation

Coming up with smart business ideas from what you enjoy

What it means

Ideation is just a fancy word for coming up with ideas – in this case, ideas for a new business.

When you start a business, you're offering something that helps people. It could be a product (like slime or lemonade) or a service (like dog walking or lawn raking). But first, you need to decide what that "something" will be. That's where ideation comes in.

Good business ideas often come from the world around you – from your own interests, from problems you notice, or from things people say they wish existed.

Here's an example

Let's say you love drawing. You could:

- Sell custom bookmarks with your own art
- Create a coloring book and print a few copies
- Take requests from friends and draw their pets for a fee

Each of those is a business idea – and they all started with something simple: you love to draw.

Or maybe your neighbor complains that their lawn is full of leaves, or your family wishes there was an easier way to carry groceries

Those are problems waiting for a solution – and maybe, a business!

Why it's important

Every business begins with an idea.

Learning how to spot ideas helps you:

- Notice problems or opportunities
- Use your creativity to help others
- Turn something fun into something valuable

You don't need a perfect idea – just one that's possible.

Try this!

Fold a piece of paper in half.

On one side, list 5 things you enjoy.

On the other, 5 problems you've noticed.

Now mix and match: could something you like help solve one of those problems?

If yes – you've got a business idea. Write down 3 ideas to get started!

2

Validation

Finding out if people want what you're offering

What it means

Validation means checking if your business idea is something people actually want.

It's like asking:
"Would anyone be interested in this?"

You don't have to build the whole business first. You can test your idea before you go all in.

Here's an example

You've decided to sell homemade bracelets. But before you buy supplies, you ask 5 friends what they think.

If they say "That's so cool!" or "I'd totally buy one," you might be on to something.

If they say "Meh," or "I don't really wear bracelets," maybe it's time to adjust.

Asking early helps you make smart choices – before you spend time or money.

Why it's important

Validation helps you:

- Know if there's real interest
- Save time, money, and energy
- Get ideas to make your business idea even *better*

Smart entrepreneurs test *before* they launch.

Try this!

Pick one of your business ideas from Chapter 1 and ask 3–5 people – friends, family, classmates – what they think.

Try questions like:

- "Would you want this?"
- "What would make it better?"
- "How much would you pay?"

Write down what you hear. Did people seem excited? Did they suggest changes?

That's validation – and you're already doing it.

3

Selection

Picking the best idea
to turn into a business

What it means

Once you've come up with some business ideas – and checked if people are interested – it's time to pick one.

That's called **selection**. It means looking at your options and deciding which one makes the most sense to try first.

You're not picking forever. You're just picking where to start.

Here's an example

Let's say you've brainstormed 3 ideas:

- Selling homemade slime
- Walking neighborhood dogs
- Drawing digital art for classmates

All three are good. But maybe you don't like cleaning up slime, and you're a little nervous around dogs.

Drawing? That's fun, easy to start, and doesn't cost much.

That's the one you pick – and you're off!

Why it's important

You can't build five businesses at once – not yet, anyway. Choosing one idea lets you:

- Focus your time and energy
- Get started faster
- Learn as you go (and come back to the other ideas later)

Even the best entrepreneurs start small – and grow from there.

Try this!

Look at the ideas you came up with in Chapter 1.

Circle your top 2 or 3.

Now ask yourself:

- Which one sounds the most fun?
- Which one would be easiest to start?
- Which one are people most excited about?

Pick your favorite and *that's* your business idea.

You've made your first big business decision!

4

Ideal Customer Profile
(or ICP)
Who your business is for – and why

What it means

Every great business knows its audience. An **Ideal Customer Profile** – or **ICP** – is a clear picture of who you're trying to help.

Your product or service isn't for everyone. It's for someone – the kind of person who will be excited to buy what you're offering.

When you know who that is, it's easier to create something they'll love.

Here's an example

Let's say you're making beaded bracelets.

Your ICP might be:

- Kids at school who love colorful accessories
- Aged 7 to 10
- Girls, mostly
- Want something custom, cool, and under $5

That helps you know what to make, how to price it, and even where to sell it.

Why it's important

When you know your ICP, you can:

- Design products people actually want
- Use the right words and style to grab their attention
- Find them faster when it's time to sell

Guessing is risky. Knowing your customer makes everything easier.

Try this!

Think about the idea you picked in Chapter 3.

Now imagine your perfect customer.

Ask yourself:

- How old are they?
- What are they into?
- Why would they want what you're offering?

Write 3–5 details about them. That's your ICP – and it's a big step toward thinking like a business pro.

5

Startup Capital
How much money you need – and how to get it

What it means

Startup capital is the money you need to get your business off the ground.

Even small businesses usually need a little money at the start – for things like supplies, tools, signs, or ingredients.

You don't need a lot. But it helps to know how much you'll need... and where it might come from.

Here's an example

Let's say you want to run a lemonade stand.

You'll need:

- Lemons
- Sugar
- Cups
- A sign

That might cost you $25 to start. That's your startup capital.

You could ask a grown-up for help, dip into your savings, or team up with a friend and split the cost.

Why it's important

Knowing your startup capital helps you:

- Plan ahead so you're not surprised
- Set your prices to make your money back
- Be smart about spending and saving

Every business has some startup costs – even kid-run ones. Planning for them makes you more confident and in control.

Try this!

Look at your business idea and make a list of everything you'll need to get started.

Next to each item, write how much it might cost. Ask a grown-up if you're not sure.

Now add it all up – that's your startup capital.

Where could that money come from? Try listing 2 or 3 options.

Congratulations – you're thinking like a real entrepreneur.

Part 2

Shaping Your Offer

Design what you're going to sell – and get ready to test it

*"If your first try isn't a little messy,
you probably waited too long to start."*
— Inspired by Reid Hoffman, entrepreneur

Now that you've picked your business idea, it's time to figure out what, exactly, you're going to sell – and how you'll offer it.

That's what this part is all about.

You'll make decisions about your product or service, how to price it, what makes it different, and how to test it out before going all in.

By the end of this section, you'll know:

- What you're offering and how it's packaged *(Offers)*
- Why your business stands out from others *(Unique Selling Proposition)*
- How to set a price that feels fair and smart *(Pricing)*
- How to start small with a test version *(Minimum Viable Product)*
- When you've made enough money to cover your startup costs *(Break-Even Point)*

Your business is starting to take shape – let's make it something people will love!

6

Offers

What you'll sell
and how it's put together

What it means

Your **offer** is the thing you're selling – and how you present it.

It could be a product (like bracelets, cookies, or comics) or a service (like raking leaves or fixing tangled earbuds). But your offer isn't just the item or task – it's the full package.

What's included? How is it delivered? What makes it appealing?

That's your offer.

Here's an example

Let's say you love baking.

You could sell:

- A single cookie for $1
- A box of 6 cookies for $5
- A "Cookie of the Week" club – 1 new flavor every Friday

Each one is a different offer – even though they all involve cookies.

The way you package your offer changes how people see it.

Why it's important

A clear, well-shaped offer helps you:

- Show people exactly what they're getting
- Add value without adding more work
- Make your business feel more professional

Even simple things can feel special when they're offered the right way.

Try this!

Take your business idea and write down what you'll sell.

Now think:

- Can you sell it in different sizes, bundles, or versions?
- Could you add something extra (like a thank-you note or gift bag)?
- Is there a fun or creative way to present it?

Write 2 or 3 versions of your offer – then start with the one you think will be most exciting for your ideal customers.

7

Unique Selling Proposition
(or USP)

What makes *your* business stand out

What it means

Your **Unique Selling Proposition** – or **USP** – is what makes your business special.

It answers the question:

Why should someone choose your business instead of someone else's?

Maybe your product is better. Maybe your service is faster. Maybe your style is just cooler.

Whatever it is, your USP is the thing that sets you apart.

Here's an example

Let's say you and a friend both sell bookmarks.

- Theirs are printed from templates.
- Yours are hand-drawn, personalized, and come with a fun note.

That's your USP – something unique only you offer.

Customers remember what makes you different.

Why it's important

A strong USP helps you:

- Attract the right customers
- Compete with other businesses
- Feel confident talking about what you do

Standing out doesn't mean being the loudest – it means being the most *you*.

Try this!

Think about your offer from Chapter 6.

Now ask:

- What makes it different from other similar products or services?
- What do people like most about it?
- What's one thing that only you do?

Write 1–2 sentences that describe what makes your business special.

That's your USP – and it belongs front and center.

8

Pricing

How much to charge – not too high, not too low

What it means

Pricing is choosing how much money to charge for your product or service.

Set the price too low and you might not make a profit.

Set it too high and people might not buy.

The goal is to find a price that's fair for both you and your customers.

Here's an example

You're selling handmade greeting cards.

- They cost you about $1 each to make
- You want to earn a little profit
- You notice stores sell similar cards for $3 to $5

You decide to charge $3. That covers your cost, leaves you $2 in profit, and still feels like a good deal for your customer.

Why it's important

Smart pricing helps you:

- Make enough money to keep going
- Show customers the value of what you offer
- Feel confident asking for what your work is worth

Even young entrepreneurs deserve to be paid fairly!

Try this!

Take your offer from Chapter 6 and figure out:

- How much it costs you to make or do
- How much people might be willing to pay
- How much profit you'd like to earn

Now pick a price that feels fair on both sides.

That's your starting price – and you can always adjust as you go!

9

Minimum Viable Product (or MVP)

Start small and test your idea early

What it means

A **Minimum Viable Product** – or **MVP** – is the simplest version of your product or service that still works.

It's not perfect. It's not fancy. But it's real – and it's ready to test.

The idea is to start small, see what works, and improve as you go.

Here's an example

You want to sell slime kits.

Instead of making 10 kits with fancy packaging, you:

- Make just 1 or 2 simple kits
- Use plain containers
- Try them out with friends

They love it – and give you great feedback.

That MVP helped you test your idea *without* wasting time or money.

Why it's important

An MVP helps you:

- Learn what people like (or don't)
- Improve before spending too much
- Get started sooner – not "someday"

Lots of amazing businesses started with a quick test version.

Try this!

Look at your offer and price.

Now ask:

What's the simplest version I can try right now?

- Can you test it with just one person?
- Can you skip packaging or extras for now?
- Can you start with a "demo" version?

Write your MVP plan – and get ready to test it in the real world!

10

Break-Even Point

When you've made enough to cover your costs

What it means

Your **break-even point** is the moment when your business has earned back the money you spent to start it.

Before that point, you're paying off your costs.

After that point, you're making a profit.

Knowing your break-even point helps you understand when your business is really working.

Here's an example

Let's say your startup capital was $20.

You spent it on ingredients, supplies, and signs.

Now you're selling your product for $5 each.

- After 1 sale: you've made $5 – still below break-even
- After 4 sales: you've made $20 – break-even!
- After 5 sales: you've made $25 – now you're earning profit

Simple math, big milestone.

Why it's important

Your break-even point helps you:

- Set goals that make sense
- Track how your business is doing
- Feel proud when you hit that first big win

Once you break even, everything else you earn is profit (check out Book #1 *How Money Works* to learn more about *profit*)!

Try this!

Look at your startup capital from Chapter 5.

Now figure out:

- How much money you've spent
- How much you're charging per sale
- How many sales you'll need to break even

Write it down as a goal – and see how fast you can reach it!

Part 3

Launching and Running Your Business

Show your business to the world – and start helping your customers

"You miss 100% of the shots you don't take."

— **Wayne Gretzky, hockey legend and business owner**

You've got a solid business idea.

You know what you're selling, who it's for, and how it all fits together.

Now it's time to launch.

This part of the book is all about going from planning to doing – putting your business out there, getting real customers, and running your operations like a pro.

You'll learn how to:

- Build a name and look for your business *(Branding)*
- Help people discover what you offer *(Lead Generation)*
- Turn interest into sales *(Sales)*
- Make your customers feel happy and valued *(Customer Satisfaction)*
- Get the supplies and tools you need for your business *(Procurement)*

When you launch your business, you start creating real impact – and real profit.

Let's make it happen.

Branding

Pick a name, look, and style people remember

What it means

Branding is how your business looks, sounds, and feels to others.

It includes your name, your logo or colors, and the way you talk about what you do. Good branding makes people notice you – and remember you.

Even a small business can have a big personality.

Here's an example

Let's say you run a dog-walking business.

You could name it:

- "Matthew's Dog Walking" – clear and simple
- "Paws on Patrol" – playful and fun
- "Happy Tails" – creative and friendly

Each one gives a different feeling.

That's branding – and it starts with the impression you make.

Why it's important

Strong branding helps you:

- Stand out from the crowd
- Look more professional
- Attract the right kind of customers

People don't just buy what you sell – they buy how it makes them feel.

Try this!

Think about your business. Now ask:

- What name would catch someone's attention?
- What colors or style would match your vibe?
- What feeling do you want people to get?

Write down 2 or 3 name ideas.

Bonus: sketch a simple logo (a picture or symbol that represents your business) or pick a color scheme.

Your brand is your business's personality – give it some style!

12

Marketing

Help people find your business and get curious

What it means

Marketing is just a fancy way of saying:

How do people find out about your business?

Marketing helps you reach people who might want what you're offering.

Your job is to get their attention – and make them curious enough to learn more.

Here's an example

You're selling handmade bracelets.

How do you get customers?

- Wear your bracelets to school so friends ask about them
- Make a poster and hang it near the park
- Ask your family to tell their coworkers
- Post photos (with help!) on a parent's social media

Each one sparks interest from people who might become customers.

Why it's important

Without marketing, it's hard to get sales.

Marketing helps you:

- Reach new people
- Let them know about what you're selling
- Grow your business without spending tons of money

You don't need to shout – just show up where your customers are.

Try this!

Write down 3 places your ideal customer might spend time – online or in real life.

Now think: *What could you do in each place to help them discover your business?*

Make a simple plan to try one this week.

That's your first marketing strategy – and it just might work!

13

Sales

Turning "Maybe" into "Yes!" the friendly way

What it means

Sales is what happens when someone decides to buy what you're offering.

It's more than just collecting money – it's about helping someone feel good about saying yes.

Sales isn't about being pushy. It's about being helpful, clear, and confident.

Here's an example

You're selling bookmarks at school. A classmate says, "These are cool!"

You could:

- Say thank you
- Offer to personalize one
- Let them know the price
- Ask, "Would you like one today?"

That's a sale – kind, simple, and clear.

Why it's important

Good sales skills help you:

- Turn interest into action
- Build trust with your customers
- Feel confident asking for what you've earned

People can't say yes if you never ask.

Try this!

Think about what you'll say when someone shows interest.

Practice your "sales script" (what you'll say) out loud. It could include:

- A friendly hello
- A short sentence about your offer
- The price
- A polite question like: "Would you like to try it?"

Practice with a friend or grown-up – then get ready for your first real sale!

14

Customer Satisfaction

Keep your customers happy and coming back

What it means

Customer satisfaction means your customers are happy with what they bought – and how they were treated.

It's not just about the product. It's about the whole experience:

Were you polite? Was it easy? Did they get what they expected (or better)?

Happy customers come back – and tell others too.

Here's an example

You sell slime kits.

Your customer:

- Gets a kit that looks great
- Loves the colors
- Finds a thank-you note inside
- Feels appreciated

They come back next week – and bring a friend.

That's the power of customer satisfaction.

Why it's important

Customer satisfaction helps you:

- Build loyalty
- Earn repeat sales
- Get more customers through word of mouth

A small extra effort can make a big impression.

Try this!

Make a plan to go the extra mile.

Ask yourself:

- Could you include a note or sticker with each order?
- Can you follow up and ask if they liked it?
- What would make *you* feel great if *you* were the customer

Write down one thing you'll do to make each customer feel special.

Then try it – and watch what happens.

15

Procurement

Get what you need to make or do what you sell

What it means

Procurement is just a big word for getting the stuff you need to run your business.

That might mean buying supplies, finding materials, or asking for help. You can't make slime without glue – or run a dog-walking business without a leash.

Good businesses plan ahead so they're ready to provide their customers with what they sell.

Here's an example

You're running a weekend lemonade stand.

Before you start, you'll need:

- Lemons
- Sugar
- Cups
- A pitcher
- Maybe even a table and a sign

Making a list, finding what you need, and getting it in time – that's procurement in action.

Why it's important

Procurement helps you:

- Stay organized and ready to go
- Avoid delays or missing supplies
- Deliver what you promised

Running out of ingredients or tools can stop your business before it starts.

Try this!

Make a checklist of everything you'll need to launch your business.

Then mark:

- What you already have
- What you need to get
- Who or where you'll get it from

You're now doing real business planning – just like the pros.

Part 4

Improving and Growing

Make your business better, stronger, and ready to grow

"Small steps every day add up to big results."
— GrowForth Kids Co.

You've launched your business. You've made sales. You've helped customers.

Now it's time to make things even better.

In this part of the book, you'll learn how to improve what's working, fix what's not, and grow your business step by step. Whether you want to reach more people, add new products, or just work smarter – this is where it happens.

You'll explore:

- How to keep things running smoothly *(Operations)*
- How to set goals and track progress *(Goals)*
- How to add new ideas or upgrades *(Innovation)*
- How to grow your reach and impact *(Growth)*
- How to turn happy customers into new ones *(Word of Mouth)*

Improving your business doesn't mean making it perfect – it just means making it a little better every time.

Let's grow forth.

16

Operations

Keep things running smoothly behind the scenes

What it means

Operations is how your business works day to day.

It's the behind-the-scenes stuff – like keeping track of orders, setting a schedule, restocking supplies, or making sure everything gets done on time.

Good operations help you stay organized so you can focus on helping your customers.

Here's an example

You're selling after-school snacks.

To stay on top of things, you:

- Make a list of what to buy each week
- Set hours when you're open
- Track which snacks sell best
- Clean up your setup after every sale

That's not just being responsible – that's running operations like a pro.

Why it's important

Operations help you:

- Stay on schedule and avoid last-minute stress
- Deliver a great experience every time
- Find ways to make your business easier to manage

Even the best ideas can fall apart without good systems behind them.

Try this!

Look at your business and ask:

- What tasks do I do every time?
- What do I need to keep stocked or ready?
- What could I write down so I don't forget?

Create a mini checklist or weekly routine for your business.

Running smoothly means running smart.

17

Goals

Set smart goals and track your progress

What it means

A **goal** is something you want to achieve – and a plan to help you get there.

In business, goals might be about how much money you want to earn, how many products you want to sell, or how many happy customers you want to help.

Business goals are like goals in soccer – they give you something to aim for. Scoring one feels great, but the real game is about how you keep playing, improving, and working as a team.

Goals help you stay focused and measure your progress.

Here's an example

You set a goal to make $40 from your sticker business in one month.

You:

- Keep track of each sale
- Count your revenue and profit each week (See Book #1: *How Money Works* to learn about revenue and profit!)
- Adjust your plan if you're falling behind

By the end of the month, you hit your target – or maybe even pass it!

That's a business win you can see.

Why it's important

Setting goals helps you:

- Stay motivated and on track
- Make better decisions
- Feel proud when you reach a milestone

Without a goal, it's hard to know if you're improving – or just staying busy.

Try this!

Think about one goal for your business you'd like to achieve soon.

Ask yourself:

- What do I want to achieve?
- By when?
- How will I track it?

Write it down somewhere you'll see it often.

Now take action – one small step at a time.

You're on your way.

18

Innovation

Add new ideas or offers to grow

What it means

Innovation means coming up with new ideas to make your business better.

Sometimes innovation is bold – like launching a totally new product. Other times, it's simple – like switching to faster packaging or giving your service a fun new name.

It could be something brand-new, a better version of what you already sell, or even just a smarter way of doing things.

You don't need to reinvent the wheel. But if you keep listening, learning, and experimenting, you'll find ways to improve that feel exciting – for both you and your customers.

Innovation helps your business stay fresh, fun, and full of possibility.

Here's an example

You sell custom buttons with cool designs.

To innovate, you might:

- Add glow-in-the-dark or glitter buttons
- Create themed sets for holidays
- Let customers design their own

Even small changes can make a big impact.

Why it's important

Innovation helps you:

- Keep your customers excited
- Solve new problems in creative ways
- Grow your business over time

You don't have to change everything – just keep improving.

Try this!

Think about something you could add, improve, or change in your business.

Ask yourself:

- What do my customers keep asking for?
- What would make my product or service more exciting?
- What's one fun idea I've never tried?

Pick one idea to test – and see what happens!

19

Scaling

Reach more people with what you've built

What it means

Scaling means growing your business in a smart and steady way.

It's about serving more customers or selling more products — without making things too complicated or messy.

Scaling helps your business get bigger while still running smoothly.

Here's an example

You've been selling baked goods to neighbors on your street.

To scale, you could:

- Offer treats at a school event
- Let people order online with a simple form
- Ask a local shop to sell your items for a small fee

Each step helps you serve more people — while keeping things organized.

Why it's important

Scaling helps you:

- Grow your business without burning out
- Increase your profit
- Learn how to handle more without losing quality

A business that scales well is built to last.

Try this!

Think about what's working well in your business.

Now ask:

- What would it look like to double your customers?
- Could you still keep up?
- What would you need to make it work?

Write down one idea for scaling your business in a smart, simple way.

20

Word of Mouth
(or Referrals)

Let happy customers spread the word

What it means

Word of mouth is when people talk about your business – in a good way.

When someone has a great experience, they might tell a friend, a neighbor, or a classmate. That's called a referral – and it's one of the best ways to grow your business.

Here's an example

You make custom bracelets.

A happy customer wears theirs to school and says,

"My friend made it – it's only $3!"

Soon, two more people ask if you're still selling.

That's word of mouth – and it's free advertising!

Why it's important

Referrals help you:

- Earn trust faster – people listen to people they know
- Attract more of the right customers
- Grow your business without spending money on ads

Great service leads to great stories – and great stories get shared.

Try this!

Ask a happy customer if they'd be willing to:

- Tell a friend
- Post a picture (with permission)
- Leave a short review or thank-you note

You can also offer a small reward – like a discount or bonus – for every referral.

Now your customers aren't just buying from you – they're cheering for you.

Business Brain Challenge

Can You Launch a REAL Business?

You've made it through 20 chapters.

You've come up with an idea, shaped your offer, learned how to sell it, and figured out how to keep growing.

Now it's time to put your Business Brain into action.

Your mission:

Start a real business – even if it's small.

You don't need a big team or a complicated website.

You just need something real: a product or service, a customer, and a way to give them what you promised.

Even one sale counts. Even one happy customer means you've done it.

Let's see what you can build.

💡 Step 1: Pick Your Idea

Look back at your notes from Chapters 1–3.

What idea are you most excited about?

Pick one – that's your business!

📑 Step 2: Plan Your Offer

Use Chapters 4–9 to shape your product or service.

- Who is your ideal customer (your *ICP*)?
- What will you *offer* – and what makes it special (your *USP*)?
- How much will you charge (the *Price*)?
- Can you start with a simple version (your *MVP*)?
- How much do you need to sell before you start making a profit (your *Break-Even Point*)?

Write it all down. This is your business plan – kid-sized but powerful.

🚀 Step 3: Launch It!

Use Chapters 10–15 to get ready and go live.

- What's the name and look of your business (*Branding*)?
- How will people find out about you (*Marketing*)?
- What will you say when they're interested (*Sales*)?
- How will you make sure they're happy (*Customer Satisfaction*)?
- Do you have everything you need (*Procurement*)?

Set a date – then go for it!

Step 4: Improve and Grow

Use Chapters 16–20 to level up.

- Are your systems working (*Operations*)?
- What are you aiming to accomplish (*Goals*)?
- What new ideas could you try (*Innovation*)?
- Are you ready to grow smartly (*Scaling*)?
- Are customers helping spread the word (*Word of Mouth/Referrals*)?

Write down what's going well – and what you might improve.

Step 5: Celebrate Your Success

Whether you made $3, $30, or just had fun trying – you did something amazing

You:

- Came up with an idea
- Turned it into a real business
- Learned how to earn, plan, and grow

That's what being a Business Brain is all about.

And the best part?

This is just your first business.

Who knows what you'll start next?

You did it!

Congratulations! You've just completed your **GrowForth Kids Co.** Business Brain Challenge.

Back-Pocket Bonuses

Extra tools and treats for your smart money brain!

You made it!

You've just finished learning how to launch a real business – and you've taken the Business Brain Challenge.

That's a big deal.

This section is full of extra goodies to keep in your back pocket (not your back wallet – those are for dollars, remember?).

Here's what you'll find:

- **"What I Tried" Log** to track your business moves and experiments
- **Certificate of Completion** to prove you've got serious Business Brain power
- **Glossary** with simple reminders of everything you've learned
- **Thank-You Note** from your friends at GrowForth Kids Co.
- A peek **Behind the Book** to meet the authors and see how this series came to life
- A list of **other books in the series**!

Take a moment to look back at what you've done.

You're not just a reader anymore – you're an entrepreneur!

Let's grow forth.

"What I Tried" Log

Your very own record of business ideas, experiments, and smart moves

Tried something from this book? Launched a mini business? Changed your offer?

Write it down here!

You can use this log as many times as you like – just grab another page and repeat the questions. The more you try, the more your Business Brain will grow.

Try #1

What did you try? For example: Selling bracelets, testing a new lemonade flavor, making a business card...

_____

What business skill did you use? (You can pick more than one!)

- ☐ Ideation
- ☐ Validation
- ☐ Sales
- ☐ Pricing
- ☐ Customer Satisfaction
- ☐ Innovation
- ☐ Something else _____

How did it go? What worked? What didn't? What surprised you?

_____
_____

What did you learn? About yourself? Your customers? Your business?

_____
_____

Would you do it again?

- ☐ Yes
- ☐ No
- ☐ Maybe – but I'd do it differently

Try #2

What did you try? For example: Selling bracelets, testing a new lemonade flavor, making a business card...

_____

What business skill did you use? (You can pick more than one!)

☐ Ideation
☐ Validation
☐ Sales
☐ Pricing
☐ Customer Satisfaction
☐ Innovation
☐ Something else _____

How did it go? What worked? What didn't? What surprised you?

_____
_____

What did you learn? About yourself? Your customers? Your business?

_____
_____

Would you do it again?

☐ Yes
☐ No
☐ Maybe – but I'd do it differently

Try #3

What did you try? For example: Selling bracelets, testing a new lemonade flavor, making a business card...

_____

What business skill did you use? (You can pick more than one!)

- ☐ Ideation
- ☐ Validation
- ☐ Sales
- ☐ Pricing
- ☐ Customer Satisfaction
- ☐ Innovation
- ☐ Something else _____

How did it go? What worked? What didn't? What surprised you?

_____
_____

What did you learn? About yourself? Your customers? Your business?

_____
_____

Would you do it again?

- ☐ Yes
- ☐ No
- ☐ Maybe – but I'd do it differently

Try #4

What did you try? For example: Selling bracelets, testing a new lemonade flavor, making a business card...

_____

What business skill did you use? (You can pick more than one!)

☐ Ideation
☐ Validation
☐ Sales
☐ Pricing
☐ Customer Satisfaction
☐ Innovation
☐ Something else _____

How did it go? What worked? What didn't? What surprised you?

_____
_____

What did you learn? About yourself? Your customers? Your business?

_____
_____

Would you do it again?

☐ Yes
☐ No
☐ Maybe – but I'd do it differently

Try #5

What did you try? For example: Selling bracelets, testing a new lemonade flavor, making a business card...

_____

What business skill did you use? (You can pick more than one!)

- ☐ Ideation
- ☐ Validation
- ☐ Sales
- ☐ Pricing
- ☐ Customer Satisfaction
- ☐ Innovation
- ☐ Something else _____

How did it go? What worked? What didn't? What surprised you?

_____
_____

What did you learn? About yourself? Your customers? Your business?

_____
_____

Would you do it again?

- ☐ Yes
- ☐ No
- ☐ Maybe – but I'd do it differently

GrowForth Kids Co.

Certificate of Completion

Official Proof of Awesomeness

CERTIFICATE OF COMPLETION

Official Proof of Awesomeness

has officially completed:

Book 3: Let's Start a Business!

CERTIFIED ENTREPRENEURIAL BRAIN

They've learned how to take an idea and turn it into a real business—how to plan an offer, find customers, make sales, and keep things running smoothly. They've explored what it means to innovate, scale, and grow with purpose.

Most of all, they've shown that they're ready to *Grow Forth*.

Glossary
Big Words Made Simple

Branding: The name, style, and feel of your business that helps people recognize and remember it.

Break-Even Point: The moment when your sales have earned back what you spent to start the business.

Customer Satisfaction: How happy someone is with what they bought – and the experience they had with your business.

Entrepreneur: A person who starts and runs a business.

Goals: A clear target or milestone you want to reach.

Ideation: The process of coming up with new ideas, especially for a business.

Ideal Customer Profile (ICP): A description of your perfect customer – who they are, what they want, and why they'd love your offer.

Innovation: A new idea or improvement that makes your business better.

Marketing: Ways to help people find out about your business and get interested in what you sell.

Minimum Viable Product (MVP): The simplest version of your product or service that still works – used to test and learn.

Operations: The behind-the-scenes work that keeps your business running smoothly.

Offer: What you're selling – including the product or service, how it's packaged, and what's included.

Pricing:	Deciding how much to charge for what you're offering.
Procurement:	Getting the supplies, tools, or materials you need to run your business.
Referral:	When a happy customer tells someone else about your business.
Sales:	The process of turning interest into a real purchase.
Scaling:	Growing your business in a smart, organized way that helps you reach more people without getting overwhelmed.
Selection:	Choosing which business idea to move forward with.
Startup Capital:	The money you need to get your business off the ground.
Unique Selling Proposition (USP):	What makes your business different from others – your special twist.
Validation:	Finding out if people are actually interested in your idea before you build the whole business.
Word of Mouth:	When people talk positively about your business and help spread the word.

A Thank-You from GrowForth Kids Co.

Hey there, Business Brain!

We just want to say a huge **thank you** for reading this book – for learning, trying, thinking, planning, and growing your skills one page at a time.

You didn't just read about starting a business.

You explored it. You built it. You owned it.

And that's something to be proud of.

Remember:

You don't have to wait until you're a grown-up to make a difference.

You already have everything you need to start.

Whether you launched your first business, helped a friend with theirs, or just discovered how ideas become real – we're proud of you.

Stay curious. Stay bold.

And as always...

Keep growing forth.

— Your friends at **GrowForth Kids Co.**

Behind the Book

Meet the Authors

Hi! We're **Matthew** and **Scott MacMillan** – a father-and-son duo from Toronto, Canada who teamed up to write this book together.

Scott (the dad!) is an entrepreneur, former Boston Consulting Group (BCG) strategy consultant, and the author of *Entrepreneur to Author*. He now runs a publishing company that helps experts turn their ideas into books that grow their business (Parents, learn more at: www.grammarfactory.com).

Matthew (the kid!) is full of clever ideas, sharp questions, and curious thinking – especially about money, business, and how the world works. He's also the author of *The Super Poo Official Character Guide*, which launched his own creative publishing journey.

One day, Matthew asked something simple but smart:

"How does a business work?"

That kicked off a ton of conversations – about saving, earning, running a business, and making smart decisions. The more we talked, the more we realized: this stuff isn't just for grown-ups. In fact, kids who learn these ideas early can use them to do some pretty amazing things. So we decided to write the kind of book we both wish existed earlier – clear, fun, and full of real tools for thinking like a **business brain**.

We've got a whole series planned and hope you'll come along for the ride.

Thanks for reading, learning, and growing with us!

— **Matthew & Scott**

Want to keep up with the latest books, tools, and challenges from GrowForth Kids Co.? Visit **www.growforthpress.com** to stay in the loop!

You Might Also Like...

If you liked Book 3, *Let's Start a Business!*, we've got good news — there's more where this came from!

Here's a peek at the other books in the **GrowForth Kids Co. Business Brain Series**:

Book 1 (Available Now!)
How Money Works: Learn How to Earn It, Save It, Grow It, and Spend It Wisely

Learn the basics of money: what it is, how it works and how to use it. Topics: Revenue, expenses, profit, giving, values, and more.

Book 2 (Available Now!)
Smart Choices: The Economics of Everyday Decisions

Learn to make better choices with your time, money, and energy. Topics: Opportunity cost, sunk cost, marginal thinking, tradeoffs, and more.

Book 3 (THIS Book)
Let's Start a Business! Your First Steps into Entrepreneurship

Discover how to launch and run a simple business (like a lemonade stand... but smarter!). Topics: Break-even point, marketing, USP, sales, and scaling.

Book 4 (Coming Soon!)

Team Up! How People Work Together to Get Big Things Done

Explore what makes teamwork work – and how different strengths can build something great. Topics: Division of labor, KPIs, public goods, comparative advantage, and more.

Book 5 (Coming Soon!)

Thinking Like a Business Brain: Mindset, Strategy & Making an Impact

Learn how to think like a leader – with purpose, ethics, and long-term thinking. Topics: Strategy vs. tactics, innovation, risk, continuous improvement, and values.

...and that's only the first 5 book! Big things are coming...

Want to know when the next book is out?

Visit **www.growforthpress.com** to explore upcoming titles, get free resources, and join the GrowForth Kids Co. community.

www.ingramcontent.com/pod-product-compliance
Lightning Source LLC
Chambersburg PA
CBHW031251120626

46545CB00007B/2756